GW01216649

First Facts

The DESERT

Written by Antony Mason
Illustrated by Brian Hoskin

HENDERSON
PUBLISHING PLC
Woodbridge, Suffolk, IP12 1BY England
© 1994 Henderson Publishing plc

What are deserts ?

What do you picture in your mind when you think of a desert? Perhaps you think of vast sand dunes, stretching as far as you can see. Maybe there are a few camels walking across the dunes, but otherwise there are no animals and no plants. It is very, very hot, and very, very dry.

You are right! That is what deserts are like. They are huge, empty areas of land, where almost nothing can grow because there is not enough rain.

In fact, not all deserts are hot. Some deserts, such as the Gobi Desert in China and Mongolia, can be very cold. But they still have very little rain and very few plants. Most of the deserts of the world are in hot countries, however, and in this book we will be talking mainly about these hot deserts.

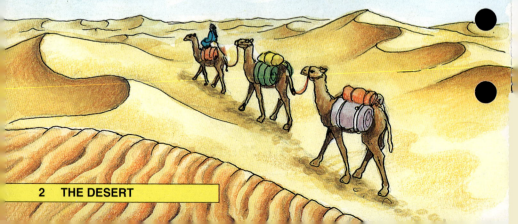

The hottest part of the world is right in the middle, around the Equator. This is where the Earth receives the full power of the sun from directly overhead. But countries on the Equator usually have plenty of rain. The main deserts of the world are to the north and south of the Equator.

You can see where they are from a map. The world's biggest desert is the Sahara, in Africa. There are other large areas of deserts in Saudi Arabia, Australia, and western USA. And there are plenty of smaller ones scattered across various parts of the world.

Altogether they cover about a quarter of the land in the world.

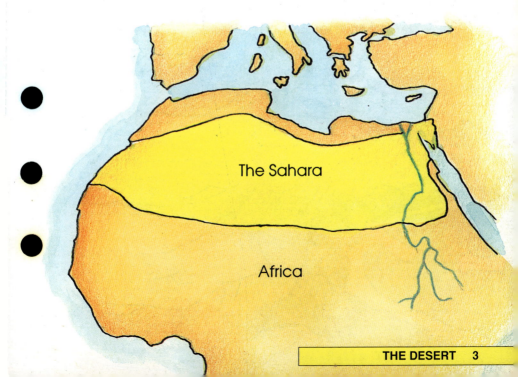

The Sahara

Africa

How deserts are formed

Plants need water to grow. Where there is no water, plants cannot survive. Places which have no rain and no rivers or lakes very soon become deserts.

Why is there so little rain in deserts? There are several reasons.

Rain often forms in clouds over the sea. Some parts of the world are just too far from the sea, and all the rain falls before it gets there. Some deserts are hidden behind mountains, and all the rain falls on the other side of the mountain.

Rain will also form inland, where there is already plenty of water in lakes and in damp forests, for example. But in desert regions there is no water in the first place, and so there is no moisture to make rain.

Hot and cold

Rain falls from clouds. Usually there are very few clouds over deserts. The sun beats down with all its force. The temperature in the desert can rise to 55° Centigrade - about twice the heat of a hot summer's day in Europe. The sun can heat rocks to such a high temperature that they crack.

However, it can be very cold during the night in the desert. The heat of the day quickly escapes into the clear sky, where there are no clouds to keep the heat in.

The hottest temperature ever recorded was in the Sahara, in Libya. It reached 58° Centigrade in the shade. The surface of the desert can reach temperatures of up to 85° Centigrade. The Atacama Desert in Chile, South America, is the world's driest place: rain has not fallen in some parts of it for 400 years.

It's not all sand

Sand dunes cover large areas of the Sahara Desert, the Arabian Desert and the deserts of Australia.

Sand dunes come in all shapes and sizes, including crescent shapes and star shapes. The wind blows the sand, changing the shape of the dunes little by little. If the wind is always from the same direction whole sand dunes slowly move across the desert. Some sand dunes are huge, over 200 metres high.

Fierce winds blow in the desert. They pick up the grains of sand, and create sand storms. The sand races along in a thick carpet, reaching up to about head height. Desert travellers have to take shelter; sand storms are ferocious, and can strip the paint off a car.

Plenty of desert areas are not sandy at all. They may be flat areas of hard earth. Sometimes these are covered in masses of small rocks, which are very uncomfortable to walk over.

Some desert areas contain rocky hills and valleys. There are high mountains in the middle of the Sahara Desert, called the Ahaggar and Tibesti Mountains.

Cave paintings have been found in the Ahaggar Mountains. They show pictures of antelopes, cattle and fish. They were painted about 10,000 years ago, and show that the Sahara was not always a desert.

Oases

There may be very little rain in the desert, but water can be found in some places. Such places are called oases. Oases can be tiny, just a pool of water with a few date palms growing around it. Or they may be towns, or even large cities. Riyadh, the capital of Saudi Arabia, is an oasis.

If there is enough water, people can farm at an oasis. Water is taken to the fields in pipes and channels. It has to be used very carefully. Water is precious in the desert!

The water in an oasis comes from under the ground. Although there may be no water on the surface of a desert, there is plenty deep beneath it. Some of this has been sitting there for thousands of years. Other underground pools fill up when rainwater flows underground, after falling on mountains, which may be many kilometres away.

underg... be reached by... Where the water is deep underground, it can be reached by drilling, and then pumped up to the surface.

The problem with using water in the desert is that it quickly dries up in the heat of the sun. For every litre of water that is fed to a plant, five litres might be lost in the heat.

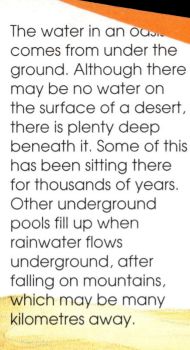

If you went out into the desert alone, you would probably die. First of all, you would quickly become thirsty and tired. Your skin would burn in the sun, preventing you from sweating. Sweating is the body's way of cooling off. Your blood would become thicker, and you would collapse.

Camels also have broad feet, so they do not sink into sand. And they have long eyelashes, which keeps out the sand in a sand storm.

Camels have bodies which can survive the desert heat. They do not need to sweat as much as other animals. They can travel for days on end without drinking. Instead they use the fat which they store in their humps.

These days, people use jeeps and lorries to cross the desert. But in the past, traders and travellers used camels. Life in the oases of the Sahara would have been impossible without camels.

Camels are sometimes called `the ship of the desert'. They carry goods and possessions, and supplies of food and water for their owners. People can also ride on them.

Camels provide milk, meat, and also hair, which is woven into clothes, rugs and tents.

Desert rain

It may not rain often in the desert, but it can sometimes rain, and rain very hard.

This can be very dangerous. Water rushes over the dry earth and down into the valleys. Because there are very few plants in the desert, there are no roots to hold down the soil. Storms can create instant rivers, which tear through the ground, carrying rocks and earth with them.

You should never camp in a valley in a desert. It might rain on distant hills, and all of a sudden your valley will be filled with rushing water.

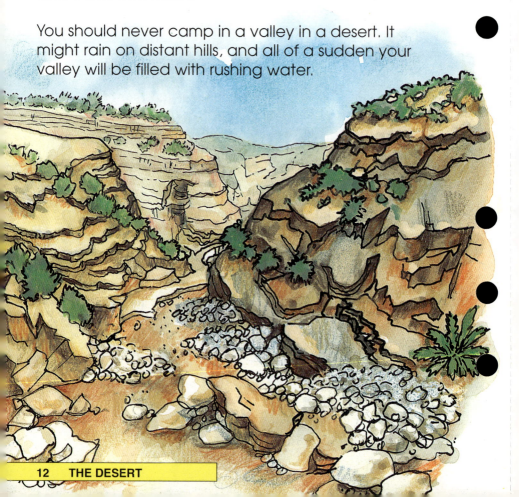

There are some plants in the desert which only grow after the rain. Their seeds may wait in the dry ground for months or years. As soon as the ground becomes wet, the seeds start to grow. They produce flowers and more seeds in just a few days. For a short time, the desert may be covered in a carpet of flowers.

Some desert plants store the rain water in their roots or stems. This is how a cactus can survive in the desert. Other plants, such as tamerisk trees, have very long roots, which reach down to water lying beneath the surface of the desert.

Herding in the desert

Some people live in the desert by farming at an oasis. Others lead nomadic lives, moving their flocks of sheep, goats and camels from place to place in search of water and food.

The plants that grow up quickly after a rain storm can provide good pasture for the animals. Nomadic herders are very skilled in judging the weather. They can tell when rain is falling in far-off places, and take their animals to feed on the new plants.

There are nomadic herdsmen living in the Sahara and the Arabian Desert, such as the Tuareg people and the Bedouin. They live in tents, and sleep on rugs spread out on the ground. Everything that they own must be small enough to put on the back of a camel when they move camp.

Life for the desert nomads is very hard. They have to survive on simple food, such as dates and bread, and sometimes there is very little water. One of the skills of the desert nomads is knowing where to find water even in the driest seasons. Sometimes this means they have to dig for water in the sand.

Animals of the desert

Deserts may look completely empty, but in fact they contain an amazing amount of wildlife. Desert animals must have special ways of life to survive in the desert. They have to know how to live off tiny amounts of water, and where to find food. They also have to know how to keep cool.

Birds, such as falcons and vultures, can stay cool by flying high in the air. From high above the ground, they are able to spot any signs of water. Other birds, such as owls, stay in the shade of rocks during the day, and only come out in the evening or at night.

The desert sand may be extremely hot during the day time. But only a short distance under the ground it is much cooler. Several animals survive by hiding in burrows during the day.

Jerboas dig deep burrows. They feed off seeds, which they store in the burrows. They do not need to drink, they get enough water from the seeds. In the late afternoon, after the heat of the day has begun to wear off, they come out of their burrows to find more food.

Desert hares, fennec foxes, kangaroo rats and gerbils also live in burrows.

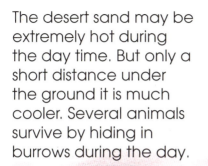

Snakes, lizards and other reptiles need the heat of the sun to make their bodies work properly. They feed during the early morning and the evening, and shelter from the sun beneath rocks during the hottest part of the day.

Reptiles eat insects, and some snakes will catch small mammals, such as gerbils. The desert is full of hungry hunters waiting for their next meal! This is why desert animals are often sandy coloured, so they can hide from their enemies, or creep up on their prey.

The sand may become so hot that even reptiles can burn themselves badly. Sidewinder snakes prevent this by lifting a part of their body off the sand as they move across it.

Scorpions use their vicious sting in the tip of their tail to kill their prey and to protect themselves from their enemies. The sting of some scorpions is poisonous enough to kill a human. Scorpions also have a waxy kind of skin which protects their bodies from the heat of the sun.

There are plenty of spiders in the desert, and many of them have poisonous bites. Some of these live in burrows. The white lady spider makes a trap door and leaps out to capture its prey, such as dune crickets. Others make webs to trap insects, such as flies. There are millions of flies in the desert, and they can sometimes be a real nuisance.

The camel spider is a huge, spider-like animal, as big as a dinner plate. It can move extremely fast on its long legs.

In some parts of the desert it does not rain for years. Some animals can go into a kind of deep sleep for long periods when there is no water. Snails, for example, can go to sleep for eight years or more.

Some toads bury themselves in the mud after a rain storm and remain buried until the next time it rains.

In Australia there is a tiny shrimp which grows in pools of water and produces eggs. If the pool dries up, the eggs remain in the dry sand, waiting for the next rain shower. They may have to wait for several years. As soon as it does rain, they hatch quickly, grow into shrimps and produce more eggs.

Larger animals find it harder to survive in the desert than smaller animals. They need more food and water, and it is more difficult for them to find big enough areas of shade.

There are several large desert animals, however, apart from the camel. They include the oryx and the addax, both large forms of antelope. These animals feed off desert plants. They can survive without drinking at all. They get enough water from the plants.

Oryxes and addaxes live in the Sahara and Arabian desert, but they have become very rare.

Desert hunters

Not all desert dwellers are farmers and herders. Some survive by hunting. The Aborigines have been in Australia for about 50,000 years. Many of them lived around the coast, but some always lived close to the desert. They could survive in hot, dry conditions because they knew where to find food and water. They used spears and boomerangs to kill larger animals, such as kangaroos, wallabies and emus. They would also eat lizards, insects, snakes, roots and nuts.

Today most Aborigines live in towns and country settlements. But many still know how to survive in the desert.

The bushmen of the Kalahari Desert are also desert hunters. They live in the open, under small shelters, and use bows and arrows to kill their prey. They hunt ostriches, hares, antelopes and various birds.

Bushmen can find water in the driest conditions. If necessary, they will make a sipwell. Using a straw, they will sip the last drops of water from patches of damp sand.

The deserts are growing

People live in the dry lands around the edges of deserts. Here there is more water and rain. There are grasses and small trees and bushes. This kind of land is called semi-desert. Often there is just enough water to farm.

But one year there might be less rain, and so less water to give to the crops and the farm animals. The grass will die off. The people will cut down the trees to feed the leaves to the animals, and use the wood to make fires.

The roots of grasses and other plants help to hold down the soil. When all the grass is dead the soil turns to dust, and becomes useless. Very soon the semi-desert will have turned into desert.

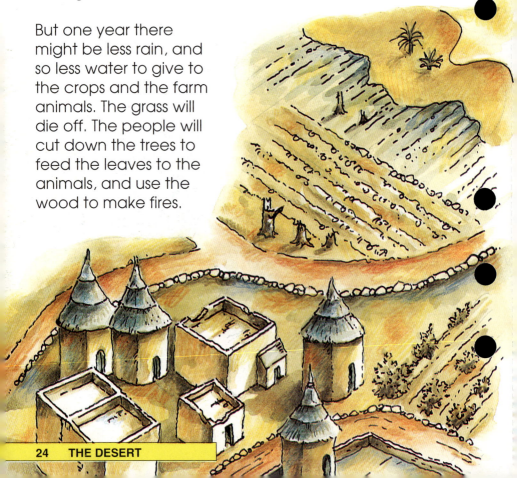

The deserts of the world are getting larger all the time. When semi-desert turns into desert, the people can no longer grow their crops or feed their cattle. They have very little food, and may even starve. Often they will leave their homelands and go to the nearest town or city in search of food.

This is what has happened in Somalia and Ethiopia in recent years. It is also happening in West Africa, at the edge of the Sahara Desert.

Can the deserts be turned green ?

Desert soil is often rich and fertile, and good for growing crops. The only problem is the lack of water. If water can be pumped into the desert, crops can be grown there. Modern, deep wells can be drilled to reach the water lying beneath the desert. The water can then be pumped onto the crops. In Libya, large watering systems on wheels are used to make circular fields of crops in the desert. In the USA, golf courses have been made in the desert.

Such systems are very expensive to set up, and they use a great deal of water.

Another way to farm in the desert is to use water very, very carefully.

Some modern desert farmers are experimenting with plastic tents. If you grow crops in plastic tents, the water cannot escape into the air. It forms droplets on the plastic and can be used again. Tomatoes, peppers and melons can be grown like this.

These ideas have helped to turn parts of the world's deserts into farmlands. But compared to the vast size of the deserts, these farms are just tiny specks of green.

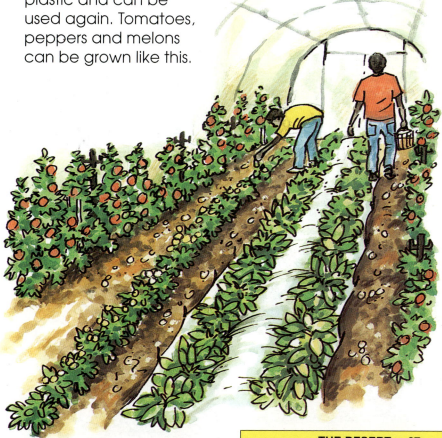

How to survive the desert

Deserts can be very beautiful places. But they are also very dangerous. If you want to travel into a desert, you must be careful. Here are a few tips.

You must wear clothes that cover your body well. The sun can burn your skin very fast, and can damage it badly. The Arabs wear loose-fitting cotton robes, which are cool and cover the body.

Take plenty of water with you. An average person will need to drink at least 5 litres of water every day in the desert.

Tell someone where you are going, and when you expect to arrive. If you do not arrive in time, they can send out a search party!

It is easy to get lost in the desert. After a while all the dunes start to look the same, and there are very few landmarks to help you to see where you are. Take a compass, so you can stay on the right course. Otherwise you could end up going in circles.

Bedouin camel herders avoid the worst heat of the day. They start travelling before sunrise, while the air is still cool, and rest during the middle of the day.

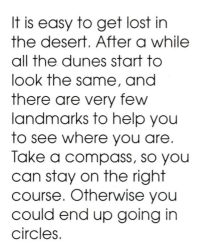

If you see an oasis in the distance, beware! It might be a mirage. A mirage is a trick of the light and heat, which makes the oasis seem much nearer than it really is.

Deserts in space

The Bedouin also travel by night, whenever there is enough light from the moon. They find their way by following the stars and planets, like navigators at sea.

When they look up at the planets and the moon they are in fact looking at deserts in the sky. Have you seen pictures of the surface of the moon? There is nothing there besides dust and rocks. There is no water, and there are no plants. It is a desert!

As far as we know, there is no life on any of the other planets in the solar system. They are all deserts. In fact, it seems that the Earth may be the only place in the universe that is not a desert.

When we look at a desert, we see how the Earth might have looked millions of years ago, before life began. This too is how the Earth might look millions of years from now, if we allow the deserts to go on growing for ever.

Words about the desert

Cactus a desert plant which stores water in its juicy stem. Many kinds of cacti have sharp spines, which protect them from animals.

Cave paintings paintings made on the walls of caves, often many thousands of years ago.

Compass an instrument with a needle that always points to the magnetic North Pole. You can use it to find your direction when travelling.

Equator an imaginary line around the middle of the Earth.

Evaporation the process by which water turns into vapour. This is what happens when the sun dries up water in the desert.

Irrigation the way in which water is used to feed crops, usually through pipes and channels.

Mirage a trick of light and heat which makes a distant feature, such as an oasis, seem much closer than it is. It is caused by a layer of hot air above the desert, which bends the light.

Moisture the presence of water, or dampness.

Nomad a person who has no permanent home, and who moves from place to place. Desert herders are nomadic: they move their camps to wherever they can find pasture for their animals.

Oasis a place in the desert where water can be found and where plants can grow. Some oases develop into towns and even into large cities.

Pasture an area of land covered in plants, where grazing animals can feed.

Sand tiny pieces of stone. Sand is made by the action of heat, wind and water on rock over millions of years.

Sand dune a huge heap of loose sand.

Sand storm a thick layer of flying sand pushed along by a strong wind.

Semi-desert an area of land with slightly more rainfall than a desert. Grasses, trees and bushes can grow in semi-desert.

Well a hole dug into the ground to reach water lying beneath the surface.